THIS JOURNAL
BELONG TO:

____

thank you for being awesome

Made in the USA
Monee, IL
25 January 2022

89802470R30069